THE AUTOMOTIVE
MANIFESTO

Dave,
You are part of the
sequel to this book whether
you know it or not!
– Paul

PAUL J DALY

ISBN: 978-0-578-48416-7

ACKNOWLEDGMENTS

This book is for my wife, Sara, and four children: Myles, Brooklyn, Elyse, and Jayden. Your love, passion, and patience have made me who I am. We're in this **together**.

This book is for the mentors who have personally invested in me over the past few years: Gary Vaynerchuk, Dale Pollak, James Orsini, Todd Caputo, Claude Silver, and Lou Bregou. I hope to make your time ROI positive.

This book is for my team who entrust a good measure of their time, talents, and opportunities with me. I'm working for **you**.

Finally, this book is most directly for the dealers, auto industry partners, branders, marketers, and company culture makers who are driven to be better. You are my people.

REVIEWS

It takes a lot to truly blow me away. But Paul Daly's Manifesto did just that. His perspective is fresh, insightful and spot-on. It's a quick read that packs a powerful, profound punch. It arrives at the right time, when dealers and the retail automotive industry itself is searching, even clawing, to find a foothold for future relevance. It's got secret sauce—a new principle, founded on the most fundamental thing, human connection. It offers an operational framework for dealers, or anyone, seeking greater margin and meaning. Best of all, the Manifesto opens the mind to ask questions about what I believe to be true about the car business and how/why it can be so much better.

— Dale Pollak | EVP and Founder, vAuto

Connection and Clarity. This is what Paul Daly stands for. And stand in integrity he does with this Manifesto. He is changing the Automotive industry by bringing care, candor and connection to the forefront of this industry, calling all people to remember and act on the golden rule. Paul's Automotive Manifesto contains Truth that we can all stand behind. No matter the industry.

— Claude Silver | Chief Heart Officer, VaynerMedia

Paul Daly does a most remarkable job in explaining the value of human connection! He does this as a result of his ability to get the most basic human desire. That desire is our quest to be understood..Thank you Paul for understanding me and everyone who has the courage to be challenged by reading this book!

— Peter Cooper | Lexus Brand Champion, Lexus of Lehigh Valley

There are few who know as much about automotive marketing than Paul. His deep understanding of the dealership space coupled with his ability to "Market in the Now" using videos, podcasts and social media make him a force to be reckoned with. I am proud to call him mentee as he is a quick study and absorbs like a sponge. A great family man with high moral values and business integrity is always a plus in my book.

— James Orsini | President, The Sasha Group

Rarely into our space comes a fresh voice... Paul is that rare voice. Most won't hear his call, most won't see his the power of his direction, most just want more leads. If you're looking to break the old business habits that bore you and your customers, close your door, turn off your phone, get out your highlighter and take a look at a new direction for you and your business.

— Joe Pistell | Founder, JC AutoMagic

Paul just gets it right. Strategic brand development, customer-first experience, a culture of care and accountability, along with the belief that customer connection is necessary even in the "car business"... a seismic, but necessary shift for our industry.

— David Long | Vice President, The Niello Company

Paul Daly is a genuine person with a keen sense of what the future will be. His values define who he is and explain why he is such a successful father, husband and business leader.

— Todd Caputo | President, Sun Auto Group

Paul Daly is a breath of fresh air in an otherwise stale world of automotive retail advertising. His obsession with brand promise and genuine customer connections should be the religion adopted by all dealers that are in it for the long haul. I've seen the results first hand and can vouch for the full impact of embracing his approach.

— Rudi Thun | Chief Operating Officer, Roadster

I've spent three decades as a "car guy." During that time, I've seen many changes take place. Not because we wanted the change as dealers, but because car buyers have always sought a better experience or a friendlier CONNECTION. Paul J Daly does an incredible job of simplifying the reasons dealers need to continue to strive to connect with car buyers on their terms. What I love most about the book is the same content could have been used during the early stages of automotive internet leads, dealer websites, or automotive digital marketing. The concepts and ideas are universal and timeless. This is a must read.

— **Matt Weinberg | SVP of Consumer Experience, Drive Motors**

There are many voices shouting that the current model of auto retailing will not exist in the future. Whether you believe we are in the middle of automobile retail evolution or revolution, Paul's message of perfecting your brand is solid advice for all of us who believe we will thrive for years to come.

— **Lou Bregou | Director of Operations, Driver's Village**

I believe Paul's book provides some great ideas on how to navigate a changing automotive landscape—so much so that I have partnered with Paul to help implement some of his great ideas in my own sixteen dealerships. Paul is an innovator who is constantly challenging the status quo and I look forward to continued opportunities to work with him in the future.

— **Gregg R. Ciocca | Founder and CEO, Ciocca Dealerships**

This book is a perfect encapsulation of Paul himself. Part bold, part humble but always with a focus on educating and helping others. The information here will help those who are willing to read it and connect with its message. Customers have "chang-ED" but many dealers have not. Those who embrace his Manifesto and thoughtfully applies what they find in these pages will be the ones left standing. Well done Paul.

— **Glenn Pasch | CEO PCGDigital**

CONTENTS

FOREWORD 1

INTRODUCTION...6

JUST ENOUGH ABOUT ME 12

YOU MUST CONNECT 18

THE DEALERSHIP I WOULD BUILD 26

SALES MODEL FOR THE PEOPLE.................. 28

HUB, SPOKES, AND FOLKS 36

A CULTURE TO TELL YOUR
FRIENDS ABOUT.. 40

IT'S A BRAND GRAB....................................... 46

FOREWORD

It would be an absurd understatement to say the year 2020 was a challenging year. I never imagined when I released the first edition of The Automotive Manifesto in 2019, that its principles would be so tried and tested as they were over the following twelve months. But they were, and they stood firm because the principles of human connection are undefeated.

Even though the reality and implications of the COVID 19 pandemic will not be fully realized and understood for quite some time, the principles of brand-first thinking and execution are timeless. I watched first hand as the dealers who have been price/payment marketers completely disappeared from the marketplace (and consumer's minds) as the shutdowns rolled across the United States like a black wave. With marketing houses built on sales tactics and 3rd party widgets, the walls came tumbling down.

On the contrary, the dealers who had built thoughtful and strategic brand foundations watched their houses stand through the storm. Actually, they didn't just stand, but they were the only structures in sight. I was fortunate enough to play a role with many of Congruent's (my agency) clients as we leaned in to the opportunities to grow awareness, and most importantly, market share.

Traditional media outlets were literally giving away hundreds of thousands of dollars in free ad placements in order to have something to run. Because we were ready, our clients were the ones who had lot's of content to run. Not sales content, but brand content. Content designed to cultivate human connection in any circumstance.

Digital advertising was less expensive and we leaned in. Savvy dealers with vision became new believers in brand as they saw the opportunity to differentiate themselves in a time when the best most other dealerships could come up with was the white noise of "We're in this together" messaging.

One client was able to change their entire business model to the lean, mean, retailing machine they always wanted. Making deep cuts to their head count and footprint, their profits are better than ever and their brand still stands strong in the local market because of the foundation they had built.

Now, all I see is opportunity for dealers. The house of frail marketing tactics has been broken down and there is a once in a lifetime opportunity to build the foundation right...guilt free. There has never been a better time to break free of month to month thinking and resolving to never go back to the way it was.

No more marketing checkers. It's time for the savviest of dealers to play chess.

I hope the following pages inspire you to build a brand that can withstand the waves of social and economic change once and for all.

In the fight with you,

WHY MOST DEALERS WON'T READ THIS

Ego and a whole lot of fear

The automotive industry is facing seismic challenges. Ones that have already disrupted and leveled many a businesses in the retail sector. Change is coming. And I believe that only about 10% of dealers are prepared to be innovative enough to take these challenges on.

These are the dealers who understand that the consumer isn't chang-ING, but that they have already chang-ED.

The dealers who have already been pivoting.

The dealers who know their customers would rather be sitting in a dentist's chair.

The dealers who are **prepared** to do something about it.

This book is for that 10% of the automotive industry.

I used the word "prepared" because being innovative is a choice, not a magic ability. It is a decision to get atheistic about the legacy way of doing things and opening your mind to new possibilities. I've learned the primary barriers between the innovative and non-innovative are often ego and a whole lot of fear.

Are you ready to face them?

For many dealers, the Internet is eating both your lunch and your dinner. That's not the problem, it's just a symptom. The reality is, we live in a connection economy.

Technology has enabled a level of connection never before experienced in history. It is a pervasive connection. Sometimes even intrusive. But make no mistake, it is the currency of business.

If you only take away one thing from this book, I want it to be this: You must connect with people. And when I say "connect," I'm talking about a much more holistic definition than typically adopted by the automotive industry.

Our value as companies, leaders, employers, and retailers is defined by our ability to connect.

I want all dealers to thrive, but I know that over the next decade, the lion's share — some 90% — won't. What I can say is, if you're reading this, you're more than likely a part of the 10% who will thrive because of the decision to pursue innovation.

You are the person I want by my side in the fight.

You are exactly who I wrote this book for.

YOU MUST CONNECT WITH PEOPLE. AND WHEN I SAY "CONNECT," I'M TALKING ABOUT A MUCH MORE HOLISTIC DEFINITION THAN TYPICALLY ADOPTED BY THE AUTOMOTIVE INDUSTRY.

Connect it with other human beings.

THIS IS MY AUTOMOTIVE
MANIFESTO

I believe we can be better.

I believe there's never been more opportunity for dealers who are paying attention TO attention... and are willing to climb the hill to claim it.

The old way of selling and servicing cars just isn't going to save us.

We must adopt a new model.

And we have to connect it to other human beings.

Connect it. With other. Human. Beings.

And this is the clarity.

This is what I really want dealers to hear.

You still have your greatest weapon.

One that has never and will never change.

CONNECTION.

We aren't in the car business. We're in the retail business.

We're in the customer experience business.

We're in the transparency business.

We're in the great place to work business.

We're in the convenience economy business.

We're in the give the customer what they want, when they want, how they want it, or go out of business, business.

You know, the same business as Toys R Us, Sears, and Blockbuster.

The same business as Apple, Nike, and Amazon.

It's doing the work to listen to the consumer... and then delivering what THEY want how THEY want it.

It's cultivating the feeling they get when they hear your name, meet your team, watch your ads, or consider your product. It's your brand.

If you think you can run enough paid search or hack the algorithm to get there, I'm sorry to tell you that you're wrong.

Remember, you didn't survive:

Great depressions
Great recessions
Cash for clunkers
Trade wars
High interest rates
High gas prices
Fires
Floods
Wars
Material shortages, scandals, and so much more...

Just to be taken down by ones, zeros, and an iPhone, did you?

JUST ENOUGH

ABOUT ME

1

If you're still with me after the rant I just threw at you, thank you and welcome. I'm hoping that what I've said so far resonates with you. I also want to share a little bit about myself and explain why you should pay attention to anything I've got to say.

I find myself in a truly unique position within the automotive industry. I've been working closely with dealers for over sixteen years, as I founded and built my first company into one of the largest auto reconditioners in the US Northeast.

Like a lot of us in the industry, I didn't grow up within automotive. I found it. Or should I say, it found me. I happened to be born into a "$200 Volkswagen from the side of the road" kind of family. I had never even set foot in a new car dealership until my early 20s. I'm a Philly kid, who grew up in a union family , and was the only boy of five children. A solid blue collar life in a cool city.

At 12 I started running my dad's local paper route (which was his 2nd or 3rd job at the time). At 14 I started working for a kind Amish family at a local farmers market. Throughout my teen years, I worked my way up in the service industry. I went from fast food, to busboy, to line cook, to server. And since schooling came easy, I was able to spend most of my spare time working.

Through it all, I always gravitated toward people. Talking to them, serving them, and building relationships. I guess that's why, when I started my first business in 2003, I did so with the intention to build a team.

Everything I have today is the result of that which was worked for — not handed to me. And let's be honest, there are a lot of good things and graces that were serendipitous blessings I could not have planned for or controlled. One of which is my wife, Sara.

On the family side, I've been married for 17 years to an amazing and passionate woman. We have three great kids Myles 12, Brooklyn 10, and Elyse 7. All our neighbors are dairy farmers, which is just the way I like it. I love running around in busy cities, but I recharge in the quiet.

The Image Auto/RimDoc team on the day the Image Auto - Dent Wizard Intl acquisition was finalized. There's a lot of love in this photo.

My first company was acquired in mid-2018 by Dent Wizard International, the largest provider of dealership reconditioning services in the country. After that, I decided to go all-in helping other businesses grow using the tools and strategies I used to build my business.

In the five years leading up to the acquisition, I began incubating a creative agency. My goal was to produce internal culture content, which would connect my team to our vision, mission, values, and each other. It worked. Despite the hundreds of miles separating my team, we moved as one. Soon we started getting requests from other companies who wanted the same. I continued growing the agency and never looked back.

The agency experience and knowledge I gained was largely in NON-automotive spaces.

Therefore, I've developed the unique and timely perspective of an automotive insider operationally, with the advantage of an outsider's perspective regarding branding, marketing, and retail.

Throughout this journey, I've really grown to know and respect auto dealers.

DEALERS ARE A GRITTY BREED.

They are men and women who wake up every morning and don't expect things to be easy.

They're tough... but they're also tender.

But even these thoughtful people can get crushed by the changes and increasing velocity of an indiscriminate market. They're getting crushed by margin compression, the Internet, social media, and a generation of workers and buyers who don't look anything like their predecessors.

So, how do dealers **survive** in this current environment?

Better yet, how do they **thrive**?

This question brings us back to my thesis:

I believe the single greatest predictor of success in this era is a laser focus on connection, both inward and outward.

90% of dealers will be unwilling to do what it takes.

The remaining 10%will be the successful ones.

YOU MUST CONNECT

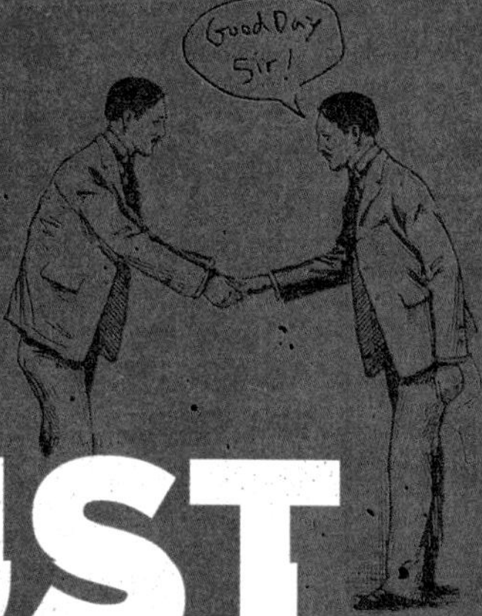

2

Connection has always existed. It is a primal component of humanity; primarily, for physical safety and survival. Now, in addition to these baseline needs, our modern society allows us to connect in much deeper and more frequent ways.

Human connection now occurs on every level. From important things like new babies, down to the most superficial of things like your friends' weekend outing, your team's latest free agent signing, or that funny noise your dog makes when asleep. Either way, social media has made it possible to generate countless touch points. All of which determine our level of connection and affinity, or lack thereof to the world around us.

You must connect, but what does that really mean?

Connecting doesn't mean networking, or throwing ads at demographics, or getting social followers, or generating fake enthusiasm for something you don't really care about.

Connection is cultivating the **feeling** people get when they hear your name, or meet your team, or consider your products, or buy your products, or consider working for you, or even start working for you.

CONNECTION DEFINES OUR IDENTITY AS A SOCIETY.

We now expect connection in all of our interactions. More than that, we feel repelled almost instantaneously by people, companies, and brands that are unable to deliver a level of empathetic connection with us. Connection is the social currency of the 21st century.

Let me say it in a different way, because **you must** understand this fundamental consumer expectation if you are going to successfully connect.

Titanic changes in technology mean our relationships have become more personally revealing than previously imaginable. Think about how you spend most of your day: social feeds, your email inbox, DMs, and even television. Elements that certainly would have had their own sphere and separation in the past are now all consumed together in the same feed.

The options are endless:

- Pictures of your friend's dog
- A new ad campaign preaching social acceptance
- A million opinions about that same ad campaign
- Your kid's school's fundraiser
- A funny meme made by a random person half a world away
- Tom Brady hocking a new fitness product
- And, oh yeah, car commercials

Our windows to the world are increasingly cluttered with just about everything. Normal, everyday people have taken over the methods and metrics of marketing and capitalism. People care about their own personal likes, engagements, and comments more than they care about yours.

Everyone is striving to make connections. The biggest mistake you can make is ignoring this fact. And since connection first requires attention, we have another major challenge. It's undeniable that it has never been more difficult to get the attention of just about everyone. You aren't just competing against other dealers' advertising. You are competing against **everything** on the Internet.

To put this in perspective, here is an example: Netflix mentioned in its 2018 earnings report that "we compete with (and lose to) Fortnite more than HBO." Yep, a new, free video game is the leading competitor of a legacy billion dollar entertainment company.

And again, if you think you can run enough paid keyword search ads or hack the algorithm and earn attention, I'm sorry to tell you that you're wrong.

Those are **tactics**. Those are **temporary**. They are Band-Aids on a severed limb.

As automotive professionals, we are in the connection game even deeper than most.

As transportation providers, our products and services are a central component of so many peoples lives. Marketing is just one facet of connection. The business of selling and servicing cars means we're constantly in front of people. Connection. Pervasive connection.

A connection that has as much to do with sales model, fixed ops, and your hiring process, as it does with marketing. Accept it. Embrace it. Connect.

~~THAT~~ THE
SELLING AND
CARS JUST
TO SAVE US.

OLD WAY OF SERVICING ISN'T GOING

THE DEALERSHIP I WOULD BUILD

3.

"What would you do if you built a dealership model from the ground up?" I get asked this question over and over when I'm out traveling and speaking. I've given different versions of my answer across various platforms, but I've never collected my thoughts in one place, until now.

First, I understand some of what I'm about to suggest may be currently out of reach for many auto dealers. Legacy facilities, traditional marketing commitments, and franchise agreements are just a few potential variables currently outside of your control.

However, even considering those who are encumbered by some of these things, I know **everyone** can execute some level of my suggestions. I'm not simply theorizing. These steps aren't a "wouldn't it be nice" sort of thing. Everything I suggest is 100% possible today with current technology and the right level of determination. Let's get into it.

SALES MODEL
FOR THE
PEOPLE

4

I'd start with used cars. This isn't because I have any love lost for new car dealers. It's because I'd want to build my ideal experience completely unfettered by manufacturer restrictions.

Without a doubt, I would operate a true one price model. None of this "One price, unless you find a better deal somewhere else and then we'll match it" stuff. That isn't "one price," for the record. It still puts the onus on the customer to do the work. It's a half-measure.

I'd be an absolute fanatic about delivering a truly CUSTOMER-FIRST experience. I would build a no-pressure, no-haggle, no-friction process that couldn't care less about the old model. The new model would live on a digital platform providing a seamless experience between the online and in-store. It would truly be "click and mortar".

I would offer on-demand, virtual walk arounds with a live rep. I'm talking 7 A.M. to 11 P.M. availability. I honestly can't believe that more dealers don't do this. If a customer is online looking at one of my vehicles, they could hit a button and have one of my energetic and savvy reps answer questions and walk them around the vehicle in a well-lit room. No automated chat bots or email capture forms. Instead, they could ask whichever questions they want. Questions like "Can I see where the shifter is? Where are the heated seat buttons? Can I see what the tires look like?" and all the other quirky things that are more important than horsepower to most people. A potential customer would only ever be an "end" button away from getting out of the call.

Most importantly a potential buyer would have the opportunity to make a meaningful connection with my brand, my shopping experience, and maybe even a particular vehicle. It would be a low commitment and high-impact process. The best part is, all the technology to do this already exists, and it's **FREE**. It's called FaceTime.

My F&I offerings would be completely menu-based and communicated in an informative and fun digital presentation. Customers would experience the same presentation on -or off-line as I would be able to precisely control the messaging and delivery through the video interface. I'd let the customer sell themselves. Why? Because the current data shows us that sell through rates are much higher with this method. It's a no-brainer.

I would constantly micro-survey and tweak the sales process on a month-to-month basis. If the customers aren't finding value in any one area, then it's gone. What is the most important thing to consumers today? The answer to that question is usually "time." Therefore, if I'm putting people through a process in which they don't see value, then I'm wasting — no, squandering — what they consider to be their most valuable asset.

When I make it easier for the customer to connect, I remove the barriers and let them shop on their own terms. The retail experience people have come to expect has been vastly reshaped by the new retail titans. People want to know what they're getting, when they're getting it, and want to control how they get it.

A while back I made a few shirts that simply say, **"Because Amazon."** You may have seen me wear one of them on my weekly show or when I've spoken. I get smiles, comments, and requests to buy one whenever I wear one of them. I made the shirts

in response to the many questions and complaints I was hearing surrounding the changing retail landscape. It's my way of answering a lot of questions at once. Maybe I'll make them available on my site in the near future because the more we think in this frame of mind, the more prepared we will be to see the reality of how consumer preferences are reshaping business.

Why? Because Amazon.

Speaking of retail "experiences," my sales model embraces this truth: We now live in the Experiential Age. We need to deliver accordingly. My customer demographic includes more and more young people — and that number is growing every day. Do you realize the millennial generation is now larger than the Baby Boomer and Gen X populations individually? And since this millennial generation values **experiences** over **things**, it's time for a major pivot.

This is why I would go all-in on crafting a Disney-level delivery experience. I'd turn the delivery **into** the pinnacle of the car buying experience. I'm talking lighting, sound, Instagram photo ops, free dinners, and anything else I could use to generate surprise and delight. It would make my customers look like rock stars when they post it on social media — and they **will** post it on social media.

The bottom line is, **how** you buy something is now as important as **what** you're buying.

Look around. There are pop-up restaurants and shops in urban centers that make shopping fun and exclusive. Carvana lets you pick up your car from a vending machine. People *covet exclusivity*, but ironically *desire community*. Consumers want to share these experiences, maybe to cause a little bit of jealousy but also to feel like they belong to a group. This push-pull tension requires careful attention to strike the right balance.

Making the automotive buying experience amazing for buyers can create a cult-like mentality around the connection you've formed with them. Most importantly, it will keep them out of everyone else's sales funnels.

Whichever way I would pivot throughout the years, one thing is certain, my model would always prioritize ease, connection, and experience. A sales model for the people.

HUB, SPOKES, AND FOLKS

Chapter 5

5

So what type of facility houses a model like this?
Not a single, ten million dollar building with all the
trimmings, I can tell you that. Remember that click
and mortar mentality?

I would build a central warehouse hub where
vehicles would enter, be reconditioned, and park
until a live test drive is needed or they're sold. It
would also serve as a centralized hub for my team to
to deliver those convenient virtual walk arounds I
mentioned in the last chapter.

Now for the spokes.

I'd lease small storefronts in the most convenient
places around town. Places for my consumers to
browse digitally or talk to one of my car buying
guides in person, if they wanted to. Customers
could also schedule physical test drives here. These
locations would be cool and well-appointed. Nice,
fun places where people could come and go as
they pleased. It would be about what the customer

prefers and what's most convenient for them. They could bounce in and bounce out without obligation or consequence. But one thing is for sure, we would make every effort to connect.

(As a side note, the above concept was written into the manuscript before Tesla announced their new sales model de-emphasizing the dealership. We have the video timestamp to prove it, but who is going to believe that. I'll just leave it at that :)

Now about that test-drive. If customers didn't want to come to a location to test-drive, great! I'd bring the vehicles to them. What could make more sense than that?! Let them see it in their driveway or their parking spot at work. One of the most effective, old school sales tools ever is called "transfer of ownership." There is something magic that happens when you get a potential buyer to touch and feel the item they are considering purchasing. This is an elevated version of that. Let them imagine what it would be like being the owner, and they'll be much more likely to connect with it. The "ether" is alive and well!

Now what about the folks?

I'd make sure all of my facilities had amenities accessible that would keep **my team** fresh, motivated, and relaxed. Great coffee, free snacks, a nice gym with a trainer, and anything else that communicated my commitment to our customers was only trumped by my commitment to my team.

But don't fool yourself into thinking that good snacks and a nice facility create company culture. They don't. You need to take care of your employees and make their lives as easy as possible. After all, they're spending theirs making your business successful. A great facility is only one component of team success. I'm going to address the other key company culture components in the next chapter.

I'm warning you, if you try to hack your way to good culture with "stuff," there's only going to be some more used Ping-Pong tables and PS4 consoles for sale.

A CULTURE
TO TELL YOUR
FRIENDS
ABOUT

Chapter 6

6

A progressive sales model and new approach to facilities don't do jack without the right people with the right mindset to run them. And with a model like this, I'm going to need some amazing, smart, and passionate people to make it all work.

My strategy here isn't any different than in any of the companies I've built. I would deploy the same strategy in any industry. At its highest level, it comes down to a simple maxim: "treat others like you want to be treated."

I've noticed that many dealer owners and managers have become disconnected from the current workforce. They say things like, "Back in **my** day, I woke up at 4 A.M., sold cars all day, and clawed my way to the top. Perks and a cushy work environment? Yeah right!"

If that's your mentality, it's time to exercise some good old fashioned empathy, fast! It's time to think beyond "treat others like you want to be treated" and embrace this revised version; "treat others like **they** want to be treated."

People become passionate when they are **thriving**. Internal culture is one place where many businesses unfortunately fall short on delivering an environment where people can thrive. With all of the immediate details to focus on such as profits, customers, products, and compliance, it can be easy to push off "thriving" to another day.

Data and surveys tell us that "career development" and "a feeling of contribution" are important to millennials. If you focus on empowering your employees to thrive, that IS career development. Thriving IS contribution. Thriving IS holistic.

> Work life + personal life = ONE life.
> The ROI of "thriving" is exponential.

A culture of care and accountability is a great place to start. I would begin with a clear vision, mission, and values. Not the kind that live on the wall in an executive office, but the kind that everyone knows, lives and **feels**. It will not happen organically —it must be unapologetically prioritized. That requires leadership, focus, time, money, and work.

Understand that culture transcends personal comfort. Think about olympic athletes. They wake up at 3 A.M., have insane training schedules and strict diets. Their life isn't very "fun". They have challenging and abnormal lives by all accounts, except in the eyes of other Olympic athletes and trainers. To them, it is normal. Discipline, difficulty, and excellence is their normal. My goal with my company culture is to be the architect of an environment where positivity, safety, empathy, hard work, and teamwork are normal.

One of my favorite authors and thinkers, Seth Godin, adeptly captures this phenomenon surrounding the mentality of successful groups of people in a single phrase: "People like us do things like this."

CONNECTION.

IT'S
CULTIVATING
THE FEELING
THEY GET WHEN
THEY HEAR
YOUR NAME,
MEET YOUR
TEAM, WATCH
AN AD, OR
CONSIDER YOUR
PRODUCT.

IT'S
YOUR
BRAND

IT'S A
BRAND
GRAB

7.

Now that we have a versatile, customer-first sales model, a facility to support it, and an amazing, thriving team to execute... it's time to connect it to other human beings.

Early in this book I said I would offer practical steps that every dealer can start doing today.

This is that part.

This chapter is arguably the most important component of the Manifesto. It has more in-depth informational, philosophical, and practical reasoning behind the concept of "connection" than any of the others. It's also the one thing that **every** dealer (and every other business, for that matter) can begin to execute to **right now** if they have the necessary vision and courage.

I'll even be a little bolder and say that the dealers who invest the time, energy, and money to develop a modern-day retail brand will aggressively and

disproportionately gain market share over the next five years. This is the crux of what I mean when I say that I wrote this book for the 10% of dealers who are ready. That percentage may even be generous. Perhaps it's more like 5%. You get to decide.
It's an all-out brand grab in retail automotive. The same principles as a land grab apply. The first brands to stake their claim will have a huge advantage. And once the prime brand real estate is claimed, it's going to take twice as much time and money for a competitor to claw (or buy) it back.

The reality is that our industry has been insulated from true B2C retail branding and marketing practices for a century. Dealers have relied on manufacturers to take care of the flashy stuff, while they churn and burn through leads and in-market shoppers with kitschy marketing and spray and pray ad spends. As the Internet has presented new solutions, many dealers now find themselves in a confusing war of data and algorithms, often wasting huge amounts of money competing against themselves and scrambling to stay up to date. It's flat out exhausting. To top it all off, the low bar of "me-first marketing" is killing consumer sentiment.

Companies like Carvana and Amazon are nipping at the industry's heels as they capitalize on the negative customer perceptions of dealers. The generally poor branding and marketing methods being used by dealers are a big contributor to that negative perception.

The truth is, we all have access to the same exact data that outlines consumer sentiment and preferences in much detail. I'm not sure why most dealers have not been directly responding to it while these other, progressive-thinking retailers are.

It's time to stop. The timing is right and the dollars to execute are there. They are just being wasted. I'm ready to help you and I know I'm not alone.

Back to my ideal dealership

In my dealership, I would spend my time and money on true brand development. Not a manufacturer brand, not a dealership brand, but a B2C brand. I'd develop a retail brand, a lifestyle brand, a brand brand. I realize that statement can be confusing. You are not alone. Most business owners I meet while traveling and speaking are actually fairly confused about brand as well. So, I want to take a moment to define what I believe to be the most accurate view of brand.

So what IS brand?

Brand is not a logo. It is not a color scheme or a tag line. Brand is not your manufacturer or any of the products you sell. It is not your marketing, your social media icon, your sponsorships, your mission statement, your value proposition, your positioning, your sales model, your people, your founder, or your CEO.

If you google the word "brand" you will get lots of results and not much more clarity. As my leaping off point, I present the definition offered by one of my all-time favorite marketers, Seth Godin. Seth defines brand as, "...the set of expectations, memories, stories and relationships that, taken together, account for a consumer's decision to choose one product or service over another."

Therefore, I teach that brand is a **feeling**. It is the feeling you get when you think about or interact with any output of an organization or individual. Do you feel good? Bad? Trusting? Suspicious? Uplifted? Motivated? Discouraged? Angry? Inconvenienced? Do you roll your eyes? Do you laugh? Do you feel refreshed? Most importantly, do you feel like you are drawn closer, repelled, or maybe just apathetic and bored?

These are the feelings which, as Seth puts it, "account for the decision to choose one business over another." Don't fool yourself, you are causing those sentiments in your current and potential customers every time you run an ad, shake a hand, put a building up, price a vehicle, or otherwise come into some level of contact with another human being. The feelings you generate are your brand. How are you feeling about yours?

Branding in the real world

Let me give you a real world example. I wear Nikes. When it comes to sneakers, they are all I will wear. Actually, when it comes to athletic wear of any type, I wear Nike. Why? Not because they sent me a relevant offer when I was an in-market shopper! Nike has earned their way to becoming a part of who I am by brand marketing to me over a long period of time.

Nike's tagline, "Just Do It," encapsulates the feeling I have when I think about the company, wear the sneakers, and observe the rest of the Nike community who does the same. It makes me feel welcome among the athletes, entrepreneurs, artists, and sneaker heads. People who aren't afraid of the struggle, but actually expect it. A community who doesn't expect it to be easy and still engages just the same. I see the Nike brand as a reflection of who I am on the inside. Adidas or Puma could send me all the relevant offers they want. They could **give** me the sneakers. I'd donate them. I AM Nike.

If you think this level of connection isn't possible with a car dealership, you are wrong. I've seen and been a part of it. I've witnessed many dealers across the country who are tapping into this level of brand connection. It is possible. The 10% exists.

For those who successfully pursue and execute to achieve this level of brand connection, there is a very, very handsome reward. Lower ad spend per car, more cars sold, and, best of all, an insane level of repeat business and loyalty. Forget the sales funnel! Brand conversions move your customers completely outside the funnel. They **choose** to come straight to you before they are even identified as an in-market shopper. Why? Because you have become a reflection of the type of person they are.

When you fight the funnel to make a sale, that is all you get. One sale.

If you do the hard work to cultivate a deeper brand connection, you gain a long-time convert.

I created a little formula to illustrate this point:

$$\text{Sales conversion = one sale}$$
$$\text{Brand conversion = religion}$$

Short term thinkers deploy tactics. Legacy thinkers deploy brand.

Which one are you? Which one will you choose to be?

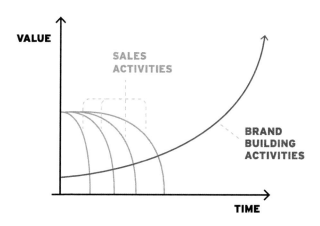

Where should the dollars go?

Now that we have a unified understanding of brand, I want to talk about WHERE I'd invest my marketing dollars.

I would spend **zero** dollars traditional advertising platforms. I mean **zero**. I'm not saying people don't see traditional advertising or that they don't work. I'm just saying they're **overpriced** and I can't **measure** them. Perhaps data for traditional advertising is getting marginally better, but it's not even close to what I need to execute efficient and precise spends.

Facebook, Instagram, and YouTube pre-roll would be the focus of my primary spend. Depending on my target demographics and market, I might venture into limited Spotify, Hulu, Snapchat, and movie theater spends (yep, movie theaters). I would also invest in experiential, pop-up style connecting points. I believe that executing engaging experiential activations acts as a multiplier to my connection velocity.

It's all about the principle I learned from one of my primary marketing mentors, Gary Vaynerchuk: seek to capture underpriced attention.

But just getting a message in front of someone doesn't mean you have their attention. We often use the phrase "**pay** attention." Well, if viewers are "paying," there had better be value on the other side. If you don't earn it, they feel robbed. In order to truly earn that attention, your content better be good. "Good" means relevant, clever, and very creative marketing. It's the only way to win long term.

All marketing is an interruption. That is a fact. Empathy and relevancy are the variables between the viewer seeing your content as an interruption or as valuable. So, I'd produce marketing that doesn't feel like marketing. It would consist of entertainment, information, education, or some combination of the three. My goal would be to **give** more through my ads than I ask.

Sell, sell, sell does **not** equate to buy, buy, buy. Remember, getting one sale because you sniped the in-market shopper at the right millisecond is expensive, exhausting, and it doesn't do a thing for future loyalty.

Not. A. Single. Thing.

You'll have to do the same song and dance in a few years when that same customer is ready to buy another vehicle.

Allow me to talk about the auto industry's addiction to having "sales" for a moment. Since I like to invest my marketing dollars and not simply "spend" them (and because I'm not a glutton for punishment) I wouldn't waste the time, energy, and money that goes into having endless "sales". Instead, I'd reinvest those resources (time, money, and human capital) into creating "converts."

Let me ask you, when was the last time you saw a sale sign at an Apple store?

But it's the car business!!!
"But it's the car business," I hear over and over, as if we've earned an intrinsic right to operate in a manner that scoffs at the way consumers prefer to do retail. The industry needs to get over it... fast.

Wouldn't you agree that it looks less and less like the "car business" every day?

The clarity is, we're not in the car business.
We're in the retail business.
We're in the customer experience business.
We're in the transparency business.
We're in the great place to work business.
We're in the convenience economy business.
We're in the give the customer what they want, when they want, how they want it, or go out of business, business.

You know, the same business that **used** to include Toys R Us, Sears, and Blockbuster.

The same business that's **NOW** dominated by brand-oriented companies like Apple, Nike and Amazon.

Businesses that listen to the consumer and deliver what **they** want and how **they** want it, are thriving. The others... not so much. The businesses that fail to connect, they just fail.

The (not so) Fringe Benefits of Brand

As if that wasn't enough reason to invest in brand activities over sales activities, I'm ecstatic to be the one to tell you the benefits of developing and cultivating a successful brand don't stop with your marketing.

Each of these other benefits of strategic brand development could be a chapter (or book) of their own.

Strategic brand development is an aligning force throughout your entire organization.

Strategic brand development supercharges recruiting and retention.

Strategic brand development makes it far easier to integrate acquisitions.

Strategic brand development insulates and protects you in economic downturns.

Strategic brand development exponentially amplifies your ad dollars in bull markets.

Strategic brand development ensures you won't be chained to one agency.

Strategic brand development protects you from being held hostage by any one salesman, spokesperson, partner, or otherwise. It transcends all of those things.

Simply put, strategic brand development **increases the value of your business!**

In my opinion, that's a pretty incredible ROI on what used to be your "marketing spend."

Why the 90% won't do it.
When I see some dealers and other companies spending six and seven figures on fleeting ad strategies and perishable tactics, I'm always shocked when they resist spending a fraction of that on strategic, thoughtful, and effective brand development. Initiatives like this pay for themselves in the first 12 months by **saving** at least that much, and more. Maybe I shouldn't be surprised. After all, it does take patience and vision. We all know that "this is the car business." Nine out of ten dealers don't have the vision or the stomach for it.

I see this as great news for the 10%.
The group I wrote this book for.

The group I love working with.

The group who will disproportionately be at the front of the pack over the next 5 years.

To you I say...

I believe we can be better.

I believe there's never been more opportunity for dealers who are paying attention **to** attention... and are willing to climb the hill to claim it.

The old way of selling and servicing cars just isn't going to save us.

We must adopt a new model.

And we have to connect it to other human beings.

Connect it. With other. Human. Beings.

And this is the clarity.

This is what I really want the most progressive 10% of dealers to hear.

That we still have our greatest weapon.

One that has never, and will never change.

CONNECTION.

Remember...
We didn't survive:
Great depressions
Great recessions
Cash for clunkers
Trade wars
High interest rates
High gas prices
Fires
Floods
Wars
Material shortages, scandals and so much more...
just to be taken down by ones, zeros, and an iPhone
did we?!?

No. We certainly did not.

AFTERMATH

First, thank you for investing your time by engaging this book. If it all ends here, I've failed in my mission. Adopt -ing and committing to a brand-first approach is not easy. It takes a constant gut-check and more importantly, a community to encourage one another. That is the real reason the idea for this book was born.

Find the others who will sign on and suit up. We need to do this together.

I hope you will go to **www.dealerspushingback.com** and join the thousands of other dealers who are committed to be the tip of the spear. Through my **Automotive State of the Union (ASOTU)** initiative, you will get free access to some of the brightest thinkers in retail automotive, a great weekly digest email each week, and priority access to exclusive events.

In the meantime, I host a weekly podcast called "Clarity Compressed" on which I work out my thinking in real time and often have great guests; many of whom have spurred the thoughts that became this book.

I hope you will connect with me on whichever platform suits you best. I'm active on LinkedIn and Instagram most, but also contribute via Facebook and twitter. Please connect and reach out, I'd love to talk. The 10 percenters need to stick together.

Please email **requests@pauljdaly.com** for any requests to have me speak, pick my brain on your show, or if you're looking for ways my agency and I can provide value to your organization.

Let's make this message **LOUDER**.

BETTER. I BELIEVE MORE OPPORTUNITY FOR ATTENTION TO ATTENTION... CLIMB THE HILL TO CLIMB IT. SELLING AND SERVICING SAVE US. TO CONNECT IT TO OTHER TO CONNECT WITH EACH CLARITY THIS IS WHAT I HEAR. THAT YOU STILL HAVE ONE THAT HAS NEVER AND

Version 2

I BELIEVE WE CAN BE

THERE'S NEVER BEEN

DEALERS WHO ARE PAYING

AND ARE WILLING TO

THAT THE OLD WAY OF

CARS JUST ISN'T GOING TO

~~R.~~ WE HAVE

HUMAN BEINGS. WE HAVE

OTHER. AND THIS IS THE

REALLY WANT DEALERS TO

YOUR GREATEST WEAPON.

WILL NEVER CHANGE...

CONNECTION.

The Famdamly at a Syracuse University football game. When we go to a game, we turn into a brood of maniacs.

Sara and I last Easter, one of the few times a year I'll get dressed up. This girl is my heart...and I look a lot better when I'm standing next to her!

It didn't suck!!!

I took the fam with me on a speaking trip for the first time this year. It didn't suck.

Mentors are givers. This picture embodies Dale's heart to teach. This was an amazing time on a sailboat in the SanFrancisco bay before NADA 2019 where Sacramento dealer Rick Niello graciously hosted a group of us.

This photo was taken at Hudson Yards in NYC following our launch meeting. We were one of the first accepted to the VaynerMentors program.

Me (with hair) spray painting the rust holes in the van that started my entrepreneurial journey when I started Image Auto in late Summer 2003.

Candid from the production set of the video series we created around Dale Pollak's book, Like I See It. It later evolved into my weekly show, the Clarity Compressed Podcast.

Giving one of our "20 Mile March" challenge coins to the youngest member of our team, and one of the most faithful young men I've ever worked with, Thomas Reeves. There are some moments that make the struggle worth it. This is one.

Me and Carvana CEO, Ernie Garcia at the Automotive News Retail Forum in Chicago early 2018.

I love this photo of Dale and me the first time we met at his suburban Chicago home. The hat!!!

Lou Bregou and I at my first NADA show in 2018. Lou has been a personal mentor for the better part of the last decade. I marvel at his commitment to his faith, family and team. He has mentored me in all three. I also owe many of my initial inroads to the higher levels of the auto industry to his introductions.

Todd Caputo really took a chance on my agency in a big way! Since those first months, I have come to respect him very much and call him a friend and mentor. I snapped this photo of him after he spent all morning out in the cold with his team clearing two feet of snow off one of his lots.

Last but certainly not least is this moment in the NYC subway with James Orsini. I met him in February 2018 at the Agent 2021 conference. James has taught me how to be cool under pressure and that there is always a solution and integrity should always be at the center.

Made in the USA
Monee, IL
16 March 2021